Appalachian Winter

Betsy Sholl

Library of Congress Catalogue Card Number 77-93267
ISBN 0-914086-21-9

Printed in the United States of America

My grateful acknowledgement to the editors of the magazines
in which many of these poems first appeared: *Aspect, The Blacksmith
Anthology, Chomo-Uri, Choomia, Hanging Loose, Jimson Weed, The
Little Magazine, The Painted Bride Quarterly, Ploughshares, River
Styx, The Second Wave, Sidelines, 13th Moon, West Branch,
Women/Poems IV*.

The poem "Emma Bell Miles" is taken from *The Spirit of the
Mountains,* Tennesseana Editions, by Emma Bell Miles, Foreword by
Roger D. Abrahams, Introduction by David E. Whisnant, by permission
of the University of Tennessee Press. Copyright © 1975 by the Univer-
sity of Tennessee Press, Knoxville 37916.

Cover by Jean Segaloff

Design by Mary Rothenbuehler

Typeset by Ed Hogan/Aspect Composition
12 Rindge Ave., Cambridge, Mass. 02140

The publication of this book was supported by a grant from
the National Endowment for the Arts, Washington, D.C., and
assisted by the Massachusetts Council for the Arts and Humanities.

Alice James Books are published by Alice James Poetry Cooperative, Inc.

Alice James Books
138 Mount Auburn Street
Cambridge, Massachusetts 02138

CONTENTS

1

2

3

1

POEM

I don't like the look on his face.
I don't like the way she begins
saying, *Jack* —it's the first time
they've spoken in 28 years—*Jack,*
I couldn't explain to her.

They used to be married.
He looks so different from the pictures.
My mother is weeping.
She hates confrontations
but still, she has come.

It is not a good meeting.
I wanted details from him.
I should not have invited her.

We are wearing thin dresses
white, crocheted, with little holes
showing our skin, like she wore
in the pictures with him
when I was a baby.

She has her arm around me.
It is snowing.
It is March or November.
The weather of his birth and death
is the same.

He watches and watches us.
He says, *Bea, it is quiet here.*
There is rest.

I feel her let go.
I think I am falling.
They both slip away.

Someone is crying.

Mother. Mother.

There is no light in the sky
behind the curtain.
Did you know you would choose?

If I call Point Pleasant, New Jersey
will the phone ring and ring and ring
like waves against the breakwater?

Mother.

MOTHERS & DAUGHTERS

I have been the mother
of a live, external child
for 10 days. I have nursed him
every 2½ hours day and night.
It is August. Evening.
He is sleeping for a short while
and I sit with my mother, exhausted,
yet tense to his upcoming cry.

A breeze flows across us from the window.
Like curtains we begin to loosen.

We compare memories of my childhood.
My mother gets up to make coffee.
All week she's been feeling uncertain.

She remembers me smaller than a cat
purring on her shoulder, then
how I screamed in the night
and stared at her too long
after she brought water
and turned on the light.

She remembers that I begged for
art lessons, and she refused.

When she gives advice now
it is through such pain
I feel her giving her body.
I accept with both arms.

AUBADE

My dreams change abruptly
from wind in the grass to wheels
on a dump truck grinding up dust.

I wake nauseous.

My son stomps across the kitchen floor
in hard leather shoes wanting breakfast.

I was dreaming of my mother
standing in a light April rain among
the greening beach plums—young, uncertain,
as in the photograph just after her wedding.

I reach across the bed and close the door
letting my son's noise fade back like traffic
in the distance, behind the dunes.

My mother tells me for the first time
about her marriage—the feelings
of sadness and loss swelling within her
as she smiled across the table
at my father eating breakfast.

For the first time
her feelings bloom and illumine mine.

I am sliding back into her, standing
on the dune, eyes slightly narrowed
by the rain falling on waves in the distance
where she stares, the curl of her stomach
barely hinting the unborn child.

Our downstairs neighbors bang on their ceiling.
My son hurls himself
against the heat-swollen door.

He crashes it open, explodes me into pieces
like a barn full of roosting hens
through which a truck runs wild
shattering feathers and boards
up through the light April rain.

MY MOTHER'S YARD

Birds flash.
The dead pine squawks.
The mimosa flutters.

My mother sits at the window
rubbing her fingernails
slowly across her lips.

I have seen her do this
my whole life.
It used to frighten me.

*

There are stories about birds
stealing the soul and running off.
Give it back. Give it back.
I want my mother.

When a good person gets
sucked out of her body
like a worm from the ground
a bad person goes in.

It's the witch who makes her
fingernails go to her lips.
She wants to eat me.

*

She kept me warm
till I broke out.
She fed me from her mouth,
scratched for food.

She pushed me into flight
then song, insisting
I find a place of my own.

Now she isn't worried.
She hardly puts her nails
to her mouth, doesn't
stare into space.

The birds in her yard
don't mean anything
except food and flight.
I watch them as she does.
Red. Gray. Whizz by.
Motion in the holly trees.

*

I sit here staring into space
rubbing my lips. I'm afraid
for my children. She didn't tell me
this place I'd find would shake
in the wind, that sometimes
my whole life would be spent
making food and warmth.
I'm too heavy to fly.

Mother, I take on each gesture
you discard. I watch you
take off. You get higher,
you circle and glide.

PILGRIMAGE

for my grandmother

1

She says just when she
gets used to cooking for herself
he'll be back.

She saw it coming.
He's been staring out the window for days.

This morning while she was
hanging out the wash, she closed her eyes
and felt her mother's hand on her back.

When she opened them
he was already down the road
carrying a suitcase.

He goes back to a town that no longer exists.
He is looking for gravestones.

And that's what he'll find, she says.
Why must he search like this?
Who will shave him while he's gone?

She eats dinner at our house
twisting the napkin in her hands
as she questions my mother.

2

That night she dreams she sees him
stumbling along the road outside the town.
When the lights of a car come toward him
he slips into a ditch on the edge
of the cemetery. Two men appear
on either side of him, one well-dressed
and clean, the other stubbled and drunk.

These are her sisters' husbands.

3

She remembers them as young men
coming to call. One leaps the fence.
One whistles on the sidewalk till her sister
comes running. *Him?*
He always unlatched the gate so carefully.

She waits, hoping to hear him return.
Static crackles through her hearing aid.
She goes back to her cooking.

At least once a week, she says, her heart nearly
jumps right out of her. She sees her baby sister
limp and feverish on the couch, her mother
slumped over the stove—

The sleeves of her blouse were on fire.
I was 14. I was just coming home
from school. I never went back.

4

For years she worked in the shoe store
with her father. Can still see him
bent over people's feet like a man in prayer.

She can see her sisters walking home
from school, arm in arm, laughing,

and her baby—the first one, who died—
its little face groping her breast at night,

but him—*He was always sullen and aloof.*

On the train to Altoona when we met—
the winter she took her baby sister
to the country to see if that would
clear out her lungs, make the hair grow
back on her head—*he was cold and distant.*

Then just as she says this
she feels her mother standing behind her,
hand on her back, saying *Margaret, Margaret?*
Must you marry? Must you leave us alone
in the store? And the young man, face bones
prominent as rocks, waits impatiently
ice skates over his arm, while she says
Yes, Mama. I must. I am tired of selling shoes.

REFLECTIONS OF THE YOUNGEST DAUGHTER

I row to the other side of the lake
watching the distant edge grow
rich and detailed.

My mother stands on the shore
turning into a speck.

If I had brought her with me
I would have asked her questions,
been too full of her life, the wind
blowing wisps of hair on her forehead,
her face mottled by light coming off the water.
I would not see the plants jiggle and sway
as the turtles pass through.

My own face lies under the leaves.
It takes all evening to come back.
I row quietly, watching for the glow
of windows, the outdoor light flickering
its silent tongue across the water.

WE KEEP HER

We keep her in a box.
We make up stories together
about each thing she does.

She is beautiful.
She ages as we do. We keep her
always older than ourselves

so that she grows and marries
in an age we only know from pictures,
her babies are born
while we are at school.

Her husband dies.
Her children are grown and gone
when we have children of our own
crawling at our feet.

We still tell stories. At night
while the others in our houses
are sleeping, we ask each other
over the phone: What does it
feel like to live in a box?

    She is dozing
    in the empty bed we made her.
    She wakes to pee, then tries
    to sleep again, turning, fretful,
    shades drawn on her windows.

Pictures of her three daughters
as babies frozen behind glass
hang on the walls of her room:

huge eyes ghostly and looming
maliciously curious children
peering into a doll's house.

MEMORY

Old woman who knows better
cries out in her sleep
in a voice she sucked from me
bent over my crib in the moonlight

She brags about her 89 years
then one night her nerve fails
she gets right up to the river bank
and can't

She stops herself, feet in mud
body lurched forward, arms flailing
she grabs at branches

Grabs so hard they break off
in her hands, clutches at others
plucks and plucks at the restraining sheets

*

I say they're on the other side.
The river gleams like a knife.
Remember? The grapes hang down
the old shed, behind those cedars
incandescent in the noon light.

We would pick all morning
then spread the blanket on the grass
for lunch.

The bridge was narrow, just for walking.
You could feel it sway under your feet.

The planks waver. The ropes catch the light
then swing out and vanish.

I feel the jolt of my body
grown ripe, too heavy to cross.

Grandmother keeps going
light as dried apples.
She hardly stumbles, doesn't
even reach back for my arm.

The light coming up off the water
is so bright, it doesn't matter
that she can't see.

When I kiss her later in the box,
it is only a statue they placed there.

*

She is across the river, invisible
as yesterday.

She is burning in my skull
like a photographic plate, appearing
more and more clear, indelible, insisting.

She is rubbing her hands down my chest
feeling the nipples. Her arms are wet
and purple up to the elbows.

She stands silent, crystal-eyed
watching the jelly glow on the sill.

She says it is God
who shines through the jars spreading
color on the floor bright as church windows.

Her knuckles are swollen, ready to burst,
her arms red as the blood that washes
all through her songs. The whole house
smells like grapes.

She doesn't talk about the stains
on my blouse. She talks about the pain
anger, the dull endurance she wants me
to be saved from.

2

IN THE CLEAR

1

The rain is so fine I can
neither see nor feel it.
I step out my front door
and am wet.

Trees hang down, leaves heavy.
The branches are black and shiny,
yet no drops fall when I shake them.
The sky has no color.

It hangs like a gauze curtain.
We use our arms to grope through
to the place where it divides.

In front of our houses
we hear each other rustling,

yet every morning we pass through
to different places without a trace.

2

I dream of my father
flapping violently on a dock
gasping thin air, shivering
in the ice bucket with the rest.

This is his death—like an old home week
when everyone comes driving in
from different directions
stuffed with news of themselves
till finally late at night and drunk
they are scaled down to the shared memories.

Imagine his eyes deflated
thinner than mica,
or gone completely by now.

I want something better. Imagine
all of them mixed together in the ice
reviving suddenly, realizing

                    the old atmosphere they breathed
was thick and heavy,   the motions they made daily
were all trudging,   and the old words—
the sayings we cling to,   for them now—
merely the dumb mouthings of fish
made out of habit. How he must sing!

      3

Some days I simply find the opening
in the curtain and pass through
to an office where people I've seen before
but whose homes I've never visited
are working with papers and machines
as though nothing were strange.

Usually at night I reappear at my house
vaguely certain that others all around me
are reappearing at their houses
or have left explanations behind—
dinner, heart attacks, the movies.

Today is different.
I find nothing to pass through.
I'm fired.

26

I walk and walk in the rain
that invisibly soaks me.
I glide like a fish
nudging the black branches of trees
out-stretched and rising.

        I ask myself:
What dimension is this? Trees flowing
above our houses like blessings.

    4

That's what I wanted.
A day almost never went by without
my knowing I wanted something.
What was it? Nothing I could hold
in my hand, drink from, read or wear.
Something more difficult to grasp,
to even want.

          Oak forest. Branches
rustling with sunlight. Green shadows
drifting across me.

           A surge of clarity.
Rising, coming up from the green
undertow, seeing the spaces between
things brilliant.

BAYHEAD, NEW JERSEY 1906

No one has thought about destroying the sand dunes.
The young man practicing photography, the grandfather
I have never seen, only focuses on the footprints
spreading across them, and the little boy sliding
down in high buttoned shoes and a white dress.
But he gets the dunes too—in shadow and light
their grasses bent, the sea breaking between peaks.
And the child, rubbing his limbs in wide arcs
to make sand angels, is dwarfed by them—
as though there are places where we know
everything that will happen will happen.

Then, movies are invented and the wind blows
footprints away. Dump trucks, bulldozers
tanks are invented. The sea comes up
to the road in winter. The rich build houses
on stilts, invent *no trespassing* signs.
Newsreels. Depression. Two wars.
Congenital heart disease. The need to know
where we came from. The necessity of proving
the dead used to live, the living
had fathers and mothers.

HIGH TIDE

The tide goes higher and higher up the beach
to the army blanket where my mother
with an old green thermos of lemonade
is waiting.

I stand in the surf being too young,
laughing as the water erases the footprints
I have stomped into the sand.

My mother and sisters pull the blanket
further up the beach and sit down again
talking, watching.

I think he died on purpose,
or they did it to him.
I build a castle and smash it—
like the glass lampshade in the hall,
the green slivers stuck in the rug.

No more house, no more Daddy, no more
Mama laughing when he comes home from work.

This is the one place you can stomp
and shout. It's all right. Things drift.
They bump together over and over in the waves.
The glass that comes back is so smooth
you can rub it across your face.

HAPPY BIRTHDAY

There will come a time (won't there)
when all the old films about eager young Yanks
joining the RAF will look foreign in every country,
and no one will have pictures of their mothers
outside the airplane factory in overalls
full of wrenches. The year of our birth
will merely summon respect for old age
and no one, not even the Hiroshimans,
will associate us with destruction.

There'll be no more copies of LIFE magazine
showing pictures of half-eastern-eyed
women our same age slinking
in front of bars in Tokyo.

Only you and I in private will remember
(as if it actually happened) the way we played
with Japanese cameras, daring each other
to push the buttons and run for cover—
or the Lugers, the helmets
with strange German names
on which we hallucinated: blood stains
demonic grins, our enemies, our fathers.

CONVALESCENCE

When you were sick
when you were raped in prison
injured in the war and afraid
sickened by bodies on the ground
and laughter rising from the boots
that kicked them, when you wanted
to spend the night with me talking
constantly talking, the lights blaring—

I nursed, stayed with you, believed
as you grew strong you would be gentle,
would see softly, like someone whose eyes
are held by delicate stems that feel
the shudder and pain of others.

But, now that you can sleep again
and work and go out alone at night,
when you come home you are restless.
I find you pacing your room, hacking
always hacking at the flowers
I placed there, the curtains.
The frightening creatures
that once filled your sleep
now try to invade mine.

Your eyes break off from their roots.
They come out wild at me.

FIGHTING FOR OUR LIVES

When you speak
your thin white face
lights up like a missionary's.

I am your sensuous pagan horde
cooking musk-scented foods
barefoot in the kitchen.

Your simple belief
that we are communicating
amuses me. *Sure, sure,* I say.
Go on. You think I mean it.

You list more things you hope
I will change: impure food,
customs, the stances
that aren't duly submissive.

A machete lies on the table
where I'm working.
I know how to use it.

But in the distance
I hear gunshots now,
bulldozers, your god's name
being rudely shouted

and I feel sorry for us both—
for my total obliteration
and your foolish hope in it.

Tell me more about this
walking on water, I say
remembering the pictures
you showed me of your home
where skaters on thin blades
cut holes in the frozen whiteness
they stand on.

HOW DREAMS COME TRUE

Sometimes at night
you do things while I am sleeping.

You signed a lease once
moving us down the block
into the projects—
one room, no heat.

You said to your friends
"We won't need her typewriter.
You can take it away."

Another time you went to court
testifying against me, listing
my emotions, my height, my ignorance
of motors and waves.

When I looked across the table
you raised an eyebrow then turned
back to the judge explaining
I should not be allowed
to speak or move as I please.

Each time this happens
I turn and accuse you.
You claim to be sleeping,
insist you'd never do such things.
You twine your legs through mine
as a pledge of honor.

Once at my mother's
we fought all night
till our mouths collapsed
against the pillows.

The next morning I stayed in bed
reading. I imagined you walking in,
snatching the books from my hands.

When I told you this
you said *No,* you'd never do it.
You shouted *sick, paranoid, bitch –*
it's these books, these books
waving them in the air.

JANUARY 4th

The house next door is gutted.
Firemen put on tanks and enter
like divers in fast motion
exploring a wreck.

They stand ignited in our windows
gouging a hole in the wall.

I had been dreaming
of a crowd swarming the city.
Proclamations of freedom swelled
above our heads like balloons
lifting us. They flash back now
collapsed, pieces of charred insulation
flying down from the windows.

It feels so inevitable
to see this raging, to see men
prying the roof off our house,
to think you and I could burn
as easily as curtains and books.

*

Firemen break down the door.
They yell GET OUT,
won't let us rescue the cats.

John hears the sirens and calls
to see if we're all right.
A fireman answers the phone.

Already we are outside watching
what we have seen so often before—
people standing back
on the edge of their lives,
people hunched over debris.

NARCISSUS

You know that time I said
after my father died I took
the longest journey of my life—
well I stared at my own reflection
in the train window all night

and if there were silos across a field
barns with tobacco names on their roofs
blurring in snow—whatever
I was supposed to see—
it was all invisible.

I am tired of telling that story
of still talking
long after you have left the room.

Do you remember where you were then?
Were you lying in bed, did you feel anything—
a shudder—as my train gathered momentum
across the eastern suburbs?

Do you ever dream now of speeding
on thin trestles across a cliff
your own face vague and distorted
keeping pace along side you
more constant than a moon?

When you touch me, touch me now,
you must understand. My trip wasn't easy.
The warmth, the solidness of my flesh
wrapped over muscles, has taken years.
I am just beginning to notice you
to wonder what you think about
when it isn't me.

SHADES OF GRAY

Suddenly I feel I've imagined that life—
the child, the husband to father him,
our clothes mixed together in the hamper,
toys in the hall, adult voice beside me
while the boy is sleeping.

Why am I standing here at the window?

They are trudging up hill, man pulling
boy and sled, boy pulling back, bending
to scoop up snow and taste it. I smile
at the details. I am another woman, looking up
from my work to check the weather, catching
a glimpse of this strange father and son.

Slowly the sky turns dark blue across the field.
The snow glows in its dim light.
They burst in on me, an explosion of boots
and gloves, snow packed in little chunks of ice
flying out as they undress. My socks are wet
from the places they have walked in their boots.
I start dinner, stirring the rice till it boils.

And as though they were sealed under a plastic dome
I could turn upside down and shake in my hand—
the hills outside slope and level off, blurred
in the swirl of snow around the streetlight.
Snow falling, snow blowing back up—
I have to look hard to keep the man, the child
from slipping away.

DEATH WATCH

You can't do this, I shout.
You smile, eyes trailing off behind me.
See, you're detaching yourself already.

I drive across the city on errands.
You stay behind to rest, writing notes
to encourage me. The bed is littered with small
packages you are wrapping to leave for the children.

On the beltway I realize I'll never see you again.
I'll be widowed like my mother, staring out
the window at dusk, my children searching each car.

It's spring. I'm cluttered with details.
I am missing your last hours, the final calm,
when the house falls silent and your face
turns ethereal.

A scent of flowers enters the car. It's dark.
I push the accelerator to the floor.
The children croon soft, repetitious songs
in the back seat.

The headlights go out. Trees hang across the road
like shadows scratching the car as we pass.
I see your face on all the mirrors.

Like a boat moving through weeds, the car
glides to a stop. Thick flowers and leaves
cover the hood. *O my husband, come back.*
What is this place I have no desire to explore?

LOVE POEM

If I took a picture of you now
walking toward me, your eyes
soft and crinkled in the sunlight,
I would lose the whole moment
like an address written down
to avoid commitment to memory.

The open door in the house behind you
would be flattened and glossed over
like an accident, or a hidden demand.

I would lie down alone in a dark room
merely awaiting the two-dimensional
return of you through the mails,
never having to repeat you
over and over in my eyes, be visited
by the sense of you barely contained
in your own skin.

What about the red car
I haven't seen for two weeks,
the holly berries just beginning to
ripen behind you in the enormous tree
through which cardinals are flashing?

I would destroy it in black and white.
In color, in plastic frames thrown
against the wall, feelings might linger
blurred and dubious as divorce.

It takes years to root out the pictures,
to stop thinking in frames, trying to catch you
face up in the middle of things
I make you finish too soon.

Right now, you are doing something
completely indestructible. You are coming
toward me, touching my face, drawing it
toward yours, so that my thoughts and eyes
which don't like letting go of things
let go.

BAPTISM BY FIRE

1

This house could burn:
books, you, our children,
the curtains ripped
into flames.

When I leave, I find myself
looking back again and again
checking the trash, sniffing.

Then I step into the city.
I cross the street between
buses with their motors
running, myself
a sputtering fuse.

2

We lay sticks across logs.
We save all our papers
and weave, stuff them
between the sticks.

They will flare up fast
then shrivel and collapse
black as lungs.

Stones jut up in a ring
around the fire, sharp and irregular.
We can't imagine the burning of stones.

The forest surrounds us—
quick shadows of trees, sparks rising
through the leaves. We don't want to
imagine the burning of forests.

3

We prod the fire with sticks.
We step up close, into its flare.

We step in then out
like children playing at the shore.

I watch it fill your eyes.
My face is burning.
What I feared has happened.

The flames quicken and explode
flickering like tongues
against the trees.
We try to run
but they spring up in front of us
each way we turn.

4

We come back and poke the rubble.
All that was useless and mean in us
lies fizzled on the ground.

We are seared down to nothing.
It's dawn. We sit on the stones
cooling, potent as flint.

We must be patient and gentle,
gentle, whatever we touch.

3

CLEANING HOUSE

I have to lean my whole weight against the closet

or the places where I have put things
will shift like a beach over night
dissolving behind the rubble.

If people don't get here quickly
they won't see the order I have made,
or me—what is left of me, emerging
from this cluttered sea.

And who is it that arrives?

My sister. A whole box of her slides off
the shelf and scatters across the floor—
black & white on an organ bench moving intently
under huge pipes, my sister beneath a picture
of Bach frowning and twisting her hair,
punching me to keep still while she picks
at my sunburn, my sister—in color, splashing
making walrus faces in the ocean.

When she really comes
she is doing none of these things.
She is standing at the bottom of the steps
looking up at me. She is smiling.
She climbs, gets bigger.
She is laughing. The whole weight of her body
is rising up the stairs. Her arms
open excitedly. Now

we can start
to undo things.

POSSESSION

This is not the first time
a strange woman
has moved into our house
put sheets on the couch, and lain
wrapped up in them for days.

You and I whisper in the kitchen:
Why us? —*It's a gift, a warning.*

She stirs.
She staggers through the house.
Can we send her back unopened? —*Where?*
Hospital, jail, the Y, ugly step-parents?
—*Shhh.*

The dishes fall from her hands.

*

She tells us nothing of her life
but the bus ride away from the hospital,
the way the doors just opened in front
of our house—*the doors just opened,*
released her like pent-up gas.

I don't know how long she will stay.
She spends the days gathering our strewn clothes
into little bundles tied up with string.

All night she kneels in the living room
her head between her knees, whispering
please, please, please, while I grind
my sweat into the sheets.

Her words are contagious. I am the one
they stuff and bloat like a duffle bag.
I say everything 3 times myself now.
I don't know who we're trying to convince.

In my dreams I am throwing her down the stairs
shouting *Where are you taking me.*

*

When she leaves
I sweep out the house, do laundry
fold the sheets back up on the shelf
where I want them.

But the couch
because it's been slept on so long
still looks like an empty bed.

The whole apartment
clean, just as I want it,
is empty.

No wonder
she comes right back in.

TRANSMIGRATIONS

the lepers

In our caves
in our small isolated colonies
where we are forced to wear bells
and hide ourselves from the world
where all we have is the sight
of each other in the dust
and the faint hope that someone
who has persecuted us will plunge
into the same misery—
in all of our private nightmares
we make love to each other
with swollen knuckles instead of hands,
we caress scabs.

No one who hasn't lived 40 years
on hot unarable soil, broken and
crazed, knows the completion
of this act.

the blindwomen

They do not mind when we tap down
the alleys of their lives knitting
little maps around their ears,
counting the seconds
so meticulously they could
set something ticking by it.
They could imagine something
stop ticking
just as we round the corner.

But now they are angry.
We sit in their doorways
with our eyes sunken and hollow.
We hear them approach, plotting out
clever, almost successful escape routes.
With our eyes rolled back in our heads
we look at them and see darkness
forming on darkness. We reach out
and touch the cringe on their faces.
They are angry. We do not hide.

the whores
It is hard having a body support you.
Having to sell it every day
then steal it back again at night
when everyone is sleeping—
to lift his arm off your breast,
to wash him out of your legs,
to sing yourself up from the mirror
in darkness, stretching through space,
then curl back in
tight and impenetrable.

It's hard hearing them laugh
when you open your legs, getting
money for sucking their lives,
swallowing them, rich and fattening
as death. If you spit it back
in their faces, it will stick.
They will be afraid not to laugh.
They will come back again and again
because you have made them lonely.

the river

We stand by the river but do not cross.
It is dark over here. The people are crowded.
We want to stretch out our hands, to see.
We want to separate and merge like shadows.

I put my big toe in, and it disappears.
But now there is a big toe in the river.
You dip your fingers. You make fingers
in the water. We splash our legs and arms.
Now the river has them, and we don't.

We are invisible up to our chins.
Underneath us women with no faces
are forming on the water.
When we go under, they will emerge.

We are standing in the river singing
like fools. Our bells lie in the mud.
Our canes drift on the water. Our stockings
our red smiles hang on tree limbs, bending them.

The new women step out wet and glistening.
Anger and fear roll off them like beads of water.
They walk through the streets unstoppable
as wind, through fences, through hands.
They refuse to stand in darkness,
to be touched like fascinating deformities.

They spread effortlessly as dawn across the land
opening hands and eyes, making us all one body.

FISHERMAN'S WIFE

I am moving silently
among the sexless nudges of dolphins,
their kindness of spirit shaping
their mouths into permanent smiles.
We swim through the liquid sun. Plants
sway as we pass. A swish of our legs,
and thousands of little fish rise up
like air bubbles—

When I wake
the day stands stiff as a dock.
Women smelling of fish gather at the square
to loom, pout, push out their hips.

Young men walk by imagining mermaids.
They love as long as water keeps us sleek.
But soon the dryness sets in, our fins
split up the center into legs with hair.

My husband says this wanting, *wanting*
I feel inside me is greed. His words
ride through my brain, vigilantes
disguised in the white anonymous sheets
of folktale.

It's the same old see-saw between men
and women, him with the weight, his feet
on the ground, me wriggling like bait.

Compassion is a swim bladder
that exploded on our first dizzying
rush to land. Extinct, impractical now,
it dangles before me—the steady lure
of everything buoyant and soft.

BETWEEN WOMEN

My best friend has moved
to another city.
Her absence thickens
the air like fog.

The pond with the swan boats
where we met with our children
and threw bread crumbs to the ducks
seems bleak this autumn.
My son dawdles and whines.

The street with the yellow leaves
spinning in updrafts, catching
the sun—is dull.

We had walked there together
laughing. Then we both saw those
leaves falling like pieces of light
for the first time.

How difficult to write
in a letter: Remember those
leaves on Garfield Street?
That's what you were to me.

How can I say
what I mean: Come back?
Leave your husband?

I don't write for weeks.
When I do I tell her
Fall was nothing this year.
The leaves browned and stuck
to the trees. Remember the times
we met at the swan boats? Well
now they have drained the pond
and dug up the lawns.

What will she read?
Do her eyes move across the page
knowing I mean: This wouldn't
have happened if you were here?

It seems like months.
Then she writes back
Winter is hard. Each flake
of snow feels like a lock clamped
on the door. I dream of forsythia
bursting along the block, and those
leaves on Garfield Street.

SAPPHO

My child wants to send a letter
that says *I love you Grandmother*
but all he can write are straight lines,
murmuring *I I I* to himself.

*

Histories depress me.
They leave only pieces of things—
a face with no nose, a statue of love
with her arms broken.

*

Day in, day out
I talk and I eat
so you won't know I'm useless.

*

Why can't we walk out of ourselves
like a woman leaving an argument with a man,
a statue
leaving the coliseum to crumble behind her.

*

I'll start a rumor
that I've jumped off a cliff
overlooking the harbor
where merchantmen enter and leave.
Then I'll go off alone,   silent
carrying nothing—in both hands
on my head,   my hips.

LAMENT

Spring
and a delicate depression
swells within you—
all this tenderness
falling like rain, seeds
onto asphalt

You drive
and see tree limbs
that have hung stiff all winter
begin to blur

At first you think it's your eyes

You close them at night
then in darkness you see
magnolias with tiny buds
like stars on their branches
incredibly distant and sparse

You walk
and the slight tinge of green
growing on willows across the field
seems more like rain
like dusk or fog dropping its veil

All this tenderness
and no place to go

You enter your house alone
hair wet, arms laden
with unbloomed forsythia sprigs
darkened by rain—trying to pretend
it is not always yourself
who is last, hardest to open

EMMA BELL MILES

Emma Bell Miles was a writer and painter who lived
on Walden's Ridge near Chattanooga from 1879-1919.
She wrote poetry and fiction as well as *The Spirit of
the Mountains* (1905), a folk study of the Appalachian
people she lived with. This is a 'found' poem, taken
from that book, and from unpublished letters and
journals quoted in the introduction to the facsimile
edition, University of Tennessee Press, 1975.

1

I felt I had no part in the life about me
in St. Louis. I wanted to go back to the mountains
and reality. That summer I spent in the woods
trying to 'find myself.' I was married in the fall.

Got so many scoldings, I've been afraid
to tell anyone I was married. Just laid low
until I had a big portfolio of work to show
for an answer.

I paint murals on the walls of drawing rooms
in Chattanooga, then speak after dinner.

*They are all romance, these luxuries
of the mountaineer, —whiskey, firelight,
religion, and fighting; they are efforts
to reach a finer, larger life, —part
of the blue dream of the wild land.*

2

Frank has been telling me tales of his boyhood,
of whole nights spent in a barroom watching
his drunken father play cards; of a runaway
on the mountain in the dark, when he, all alone
at twelve years, guided the team home
through the burning woods.

I was educated on Harper's Magazine.
I drew, read, wrote a little.

> *Who knows him? Who has tracked him*
> *to that wild, remote spot, echo-haunted,*
> *beautiful, terrible, where he dwells?*

3

We live so far apart we rarely see more
than the blue smoke of each other's chimney.

A woman during the month sees hardly a face
outside her family.

I know of no one who reads
Thoreau except my husband.
We discovered him ourselves
quite by accident.

Today I painted 14 of those confounded
little landscapes, wretched daubs
of souvenirs.

4

Frank has been telling me
of his early acquaintance with all the vice
in the lowest dives of Chattanooga.

I have papered the main room with two coats
of newspaper, adding greatly to its comfort,
light, and cleanliness.

At twenty the mountain woman is old
in all that makes a woman old —toil, sorrow,
childbearing, loneliness, and want.

I have used my last stretcher of canvas.

5

Men do not live in the house. They come in
to eat and sleep, but their life is outdoors,
the excitement of fighting and journeying,
of wild rides and nights of danger.

That lewd and drunken crew.

I've been afraid to tell anyone.

They are so silent.

I wrote

Thus a rift is set between the sexes

His ambition leads him to make drain after drain
on the strength of his silent, wingless mate

The woman's experience is the deeper

She gains the courage of the fatalist

Her strength and endurance are beyond imagination
to women of the sheltered life.

6

I hate him lewd and drunken. Tobacco stains
and stale perspiration.

I write to my friend in New England,

"It is quite different here in the mountains,
where the traditions, while of deep import
and interest and capable of giving rise
to a literature are, so far, anything
but literary."

7

I have used my last stretcher
capable of giving rise
to a literature.

No one reads Thoreau.

In Chattanooga they say I have
thrown my life away.

I write of the mountains, the finer,
larger dream, the mountain in the dark—

Who has ever understood

that wild, remote spot

through the burning woods

we discovered ourselves

beautiful, terrible

by accident?

LOT'S WIFE

Skyline of mausoleums! The city is gone.

I thought if I cried
the hot tears would loosen me.

Instead I packed myself further—
thin streams of salt running down
like candle wax.

All I saw was the whiteness closing in.
Lot! The sky is falling.

His shoulders wrenched violently
but he kept on walking, muttering
let go, let go.

Lot! My whole life was in that city.

My body pulled two ways at once.
I was covered with sweat.
Tears jam my eyes, solidified.
Black after-images fall like grit.

Nothing in the valley absorbs my grief.
The brine within seeps out and crusts
to a skin-tight mold.

This salt burns. Vegetation dies
in widening circles.

Lot and my daughters repeople the mountains
with children in whom my blood is thinned
and thinned again each generation
until only traces of bitterness remain.

My children, my children—
Do you cry fresh water?
Do your lives flow like rivers in spring
clutching at nothing, so obedient to God
there is no sting in your flesh,
no curse in your preservation?

ALCHEMY

—My sister is annoyed by this foolishness.

Still, she herself would like to be
precious in her field, striking gold
from the jackhammer noises of our lives.
She enters the dark organ chambers
like a miner, searching for new sound.

She sits beside me in the car headed south
across state lines, telling me I will learn
to be happy.

I tell her: Everything dreams of itself
transmuted. Lead yearns to flow. Water wants
to rise up its banks and seep like air
through the pores of all living things.
Wind dreams of solidity.
It pictures itself as leaves shimmering.

Martha, the trees this autumn catch
and burst across the mountains. Your voice
burns in my mind for days after you leave.

When I hear your music bursting its pipes,
the old scales fallen away, I picture sparks
jumping from person to person in a crowd
till we're all ignited.

Then I am back in my separate house
watching the trees char at dusk.

The beauty I want, the strength, endurance
take so painfully long, I feel like coal
lying in a dark bed, tightening itself
into diamond.

JEPHTHAH'S DAUGHTER

> And Jephthah vowed to the Lord: If you will
> deliver the children of Ammon into my hands,
> then whatever comes out of my house to meet
> me when I return in peace, I will offer up as a
> burnt offering.
>
> Judges 11: 30, 31

I came out with timbrels and dancing
to greet you.

When I saw you draw close, I ran
waving my arms through the air.
You stopped, frozen in place.

Then you were tearing your clothes
crying and crying, *My daughter*
you have brought me very low.

All I could ask for were two months
to mourn, to surround myself with
young women and wander the hillsides
till the shock left my body.

You I would run from, Father
your only child, renouncing the rashness
of your mouth, your war-hardened face
now black with ashes.

But all summer I've watched the grass
wither and brown across the mountains
until even in sleep there's no running
from God.

My companions weep for this sad compliance,
my womb no child will unlock, arms
that will never loosen and ripple with age.

Their sobbing swells and diminishes behind me
like wind passing to the far edge of a field.

All across these mountains, the wheat has burst
into seed. It bows to the harvester's hand.

I am the unblemished sacrifice
slowly moving down these hills to the altar.

The sun streaks through my hair.
The lost green of the mountains pulses
in my eyes. My fingers are translucent.

All summer God has flashed before me
in the brief life-spans of dragonflies
and moths. Already he has lifted me
out of this hunger, my body.

APPALACHIAN WINTER

1

I sit in darkness
beside the stove, rocking

like Gretel come back alone
to the old, tight place—
away from her father and brother now,
lonely as the witch herself.

I stoke the fire.

When I close my eyes
the forest returns. Flickers of trail
disappear like snakes under rocks,
ledges drop sudden as guillotines.

I see that others who came here before me
have left no more of themselves than
pieces of chimney crumbling like bread.

2

The change I want I cannot name—
perhaps the ability to live anywhere
not fearing the little shacks
scattered throughout the hollows
where women stare, grim with silence,
growing thinner each year.

I have crawled through briars
until I cannot recognize
the woman on my face.

I have cut stems, set stalks on fire.
Nights I dream of luring children
to join me.

3

These mountains were opened by men
unashamed of slaughter, mapped
by the crisscrossing of bootleggers.
Now night after night, they are held in place
by women left alone, aging too quickly in shacks,
their shotguns pointed at shadows.

Something rustles at my window.

Hansel? Hansel?
I rummage the sheets all night.

In the morning I pull out the vines
that brush and scrape against the glass.
I sift dirt through my fingers.
Learn not to hate myself.

Hansel. Hansel. I continue
to speak out loud for months.

4

When our new mother moved in
she stood in the doorway
staring at the forest that held her
like a madwoman screaming in the attic.
Her face was so hard, Hansel and I
broke just looking at her.

We took off through the flickering of leaves.

At each cabin we came to
she appeared before us, grim, hungry.

Father was a woodsman. He taught us
to cut down everything in our paths
till we were left standing in a clearing.

5

Later, we played house. Hansel deepened
his voice and disappeared through the trees.
He left me raising mine
to screech at our imaginary children
till my face was stiff.

Once I thought I could live forever
tip-toeing on the edge of his shadow.
I tried to burn down the woods for him.

Now I tie bright cloth to branches,
hike in further and further.

Hansel! Do you hear me? I walk alone.
The bushes do not jump out and grab.
I shed layers of anger and fear
as easily as leaves falling
first from the maples on the ridge,
then in flame-colored waves moving down.

6

The sun rises. The ridge
separates itself from the sky,
comes forward with what scant color
the cold has left it.

I see that land has tides.
Our mother sank. The dirt closed over her.
But the waves of disturbance
did not spread out and fade as on water.

Father was the last part of her
I clung to—last root of the pain
that swelled within her, crying
for a life of its own.
I cannot go home.

7

I cut, trowel,
burn my roots like fuses.
I belong in this strip-mined land.

Perhaps it's her death I fear—
that body shriveling before me.

I turned and ran. The flames grew
smaller through the leaves.

Her voice cracked like dry wood.
It hissed, licked through my thoughts.

Now it is gone, that hunger
scorching the tree limbs black.

I heat my oven with sticks.
It is not so hard after all
to keep from burning myself,
to forgive the lonely women
whose love curdled inside me.

As the day warms, I open the house
and step outdoors. Rocking on this porch
rooted in mountains, I stare across the ridge
singing the old hymns I've learned here,
words that say there is nothing to fear.